DIVORCE

A to Z

A Quick Look
at the First Year

SARAH FLAKE

Illustrations by Annie Poon

Copyright © 2019 Sarah Flake

Author: Sarah Flake
Title: Divorce A to Z: A Quick Look at the First Year

Art by Annie Poon
Design by Jana Rade

Hardback ISBN: 978-1-7330866-0-8
eBook ISBN: 978-1-7330866-1-5

www.sarahflake.com

Introduction

Whether you're just contemplating the possibility of divorce or are actively going through the process, this is probably an incredibly difficult time in your life, and you may be feeling scared or lost. This publication intends to provide you with solidarity and advice for situations and feelings you are likely to face in the first year or so after your divorce.

I wrote this through the lens of my personal experience and understand that every situation is unique. Though some of this may not apply to you individually, feel free to translate my intent to your unique story as you move forward into this new phase of your life. This publication isn't about blaming or shaming any parties involved. It is about what the post-divorce experience might look like as you move forward. Your feelings are valid. You are valid. I hope my book gifts to you this assurance.

At a Glance:

A is for Aftermath

B is for Bare

C is for Cats

D is for Darling

E is for Empty

F is for Friends

G is for Gossip

H is for Hobbies

I is for I

J is for Jogging

K is for Kisses

L is for Loneliness

M is for Money

N is for Noise

O is for Oasis

P is for Pacing

Q is for Questions

R is for Restraint

S is for Single

T is for Tinder

U is for Underwear

V is for Victory

W is for Wishes

X is for Xanax

Y is for Yes

Z is for Zero

A is for Aftermath

You're curled up in some temporary rental apartment with popcorn ceilings, wildly screaming into a room full of unpacked boxes, clutching your head and sobbing like you've never sobbed before. Knowing you're doing something hard, accept that you are going to feel any emotion at any time during this initial period. You could be laughing one second and screaming the next. Things are going to pop up all around you and trigger intense emotions.

Regardless of who did what, it's surreal to find yourself actually at this point. Your tears may have nothing to do with whether the divorce was "right or wrong" and everything to do with the huge upheaval you've just experienced in your life. Let yourself feel whatever you need to feel right now. Accept that it's going to be messy.

B is for Bare

It only weighed a few grams, but that wedding ring is conspicuously gone. Somehow the loss of just this small weight throws your entire body off balance. Your left arm now feels weightless, and you get a slight feeling of vertigo when you think about it. You walk through the grocery store with your two hands clutching the shopping cart, wondering if the people passing you in the aisles are as aware of your bare finger as you are. Will they treat you differently?

For so long that ring was a comforting reassurance of what your future years might look like. You had only to gently rub a thumb over it during tough times to remind yourself that you had invested in happiness and stability, then worries of the future would dissipate. It had felt like your trusty anchor in the choppy bay. Your North Star. Or was it more like Dumbo's Magic Feather? Now when you find yourself rubbing your thumb over that bare spot, your future manifests as only a thick, gray fog. Nothing is written for you anymore. Come to think of it, was it ever? Depending on the day, this is either massively terrifying or exhilarating beyond measure.

C is for Cats

This could be a really lovely time for you to adopt a buddy to share your space. Cats do make entertaining, cozy housemates. Fine, so maybe you're not a cat person. A dog, fish, gecko, pet worm, any other living creature you can take care of, talk to, hold, be responsible for, will serve the same purpose right now of focusing on life's simple pleasures. Feel free to vent to Mr. Squiggles when you're feeling alone, and take comfort in knowing that if you can manage to keep this little critter alive, you can probably stay afloat as well. You will discover how simple daily needs really can be: food, water, a safe space to sleep.

Studies show that when you stroke an animal, your body releases relaxation hormones, reduces stress hormones, and lowers blood pressure. If you can't find the motivation to take a walk yourself, an eager dog might just be that reason you need to get outside and see the sun today. Consider adopting an animal into your world right now. The more potential that new life has for loving you back, the more fulfilling this partnership will be. Not sure you're in a good place for the commitment? Contact a local shelter and see about taking in a furry roommate on a foster-care basis.

D is for Darling

You may solidly hate each other at this point, but for some reason, you can't stop calling your ex "darling" or "babe" or "Boo Bear" out of habit when you're on the phone or chatting briefly during a child custody exchange or legal issue. Calling them by their given name is one more new habit you haven't quite developed yet. It will come, but dammit, did you really just call him "honey" again when you saw him at the courthouse?

Don't assume this is some manifestation of inner truth that you are still soulmates and shouldn't have split up. It's just a habit, just like still making enough coffee for two in the morning is just a habit. Don't let it throw you. Habits can be broken, your ex has a name, and you'll figure it out soon enough.

E is for Empty

There is a huge, gaping void where your marriage was, and the emptiness of this space screams for your attention. It's okay; you can look into this black nothing and hopefully will see the new space for your growth. What else in your life can be swept aside to create more room for fresh roots? Do you have any other relationships or commitments that are keeping you from really being in touch with your best self or are unnecessarily draining your energy? Do you really need to be on that neighborhood committee, or are you just participating to please someone else or to manufacture an idealized social perception? How many of your coffee mugs do you really need to hold on to right now? Which of your belongings just keep you busy or financially stressed by maintaining them?

This is a great time to downsize, take out the trash, cut out the extra people, activities, and possessions that don't serve your ultimate goal. Delete the apps or social media that you're using to fill in those blank moments of your day and are keeping you from having to face your present reality. Don't be afraid of the still, empty times. Use them to plan for your growth.

F is for Friends

You know who they are now. The ones who actually call. They want to spend time with you even though you can't couples-date with them anymore. They are the ones who drag you out for lunch or coffee and allow you to have full mental breakdowns over something you saw on social media or a surprisingly poignant car commercial. You will have days when you don't want contact; no witnesses to the chaos that is your life right now. But the days when you choose to let friends in always end up feeling better.

The good friends don't want details, they don't want updates. The good friends just offer loving reminders that you are not alone. You wonder if you'll ever be as good a friend as they are and hope you will. Even if you don't respond to their supportive text right away, you mentally file their name away as "one of the good ones." On a better day, you'll be able to gratefully reach out, knowing you've got someone to listen. But you don't have to keep them all. Watch out for the ones who try to drag you into destructive habits like excessive drinking or substance abuse. A friend you don't need drugs or alcohol to enjoy time with is worth their weight in gold. It only takes a handful of quality people in your life to satisfy that social itch. Curate your friends' group carefully and only hang out with those who are mutually enriching.

G is for Gossip

You can't stop them - people are going to talk. Trust me, no matter what you do or don't say, everyone will have their own idea of what went wrong or who is to blame in your divorce. Listen closely; you cannot control the gossip. Please release any idea that you need to control the narrative. Any attempts will only throw gas on the dumpster fire. The only people who will understand the situation are you and your ex. Efforts to try and communicate an entire relationship and marriage worth of experiences will be futile. Relax. Let them gossip. Don't give them any additional fuel. Rise above and know that what people say does not affect the actual truth. You are under no obligation to react or respond to the idle gossip of the masses.

The silver lining of gossip is that it will reveal to you those who are unworthy of your confidences in the future. People tend to be self-sorting that way. Save your energy to deal with things you can control.

H is for Hobbies

It's time to dig up an old one or create some new ones. Does your day now start by practicing that new song you like on the guitar? Ever wanted to learn French to inspire a future trip overseas? There are no dogs too old, and there are always new tricks! Look for community classes, meetup groups, YouTube tutorials. Discover how amazing it is to work hard at learning something

new just for the joy of it. Finally mastered folding that origami crane? Of course, you did! Now, what else can you do? You are keeping your brain engaged, creating, and achieving. This is a much better mental state than being stuck in thoughts of the past or dwelling on things in your life that have not gone to plan.

One of the great benefits of a hobby is that you'll be able to connect in person or online with a universe of other people who share your same passion. So break out that trombone, your snowshoes, that sketchpad, your unicycle and have some fun.

I is for I

You are an "I" now. Actually, the big secret is you were an "I" all along, but somewhere along the way you forgot this and thought of yourself exclusively as a "We." A "They." An "Us." You may even still refer to yourself as "We" when talking to others for months after the separation. Don't let this phase you. Get to know yourself again. This is going to sound cheesy, but there really is "The One" and it's been you all along. Until you internalize this, you're always going to feel like you're coming up short when you look for validation and completion in other people. Take a moment to tell yourself five reasons why you are an incredible person. Write a list of all the things you have accomplished in life that you're proud of. Next time you go to the restroom, give yourself a hug and an encouraging smile in the mirror on your way out.

Take a moment to look into your eyes, red and tired as they may be, and love the hell out of that person because they really need it right now. You know what could be fun? Take yourself on a date! Treat yourself to a night at the theater and the rotating sushi bar. Pamper yourself in the way only you know how. Try saying "I love you" to yourself first thing in the morning or when you're having a hard moment. Your value is not based on your relationship to anyone else. You are complete as you are.

J is for Jogging

Actually, strike that. Even divorce won't make jogging easier. Let's make J for Joking instead. Look up a daily joke online - something to put a smile on your face, a laugh to loosen up your tight chest. You might not run into anything funny today unless you intentionally set out looking for it. Find a joke website or forum that you check frequently, or have pop up on your phone daily. Just find something to laugh about. Knock knock jokes, blonde jokes, math jokes, cats-being-jerks memes, whatever strikes your fancy. Hey, here's a joke for you, what do you call a woman who's lost 95% of her intelligence? Divorced! Just laugh already.

To gain some sense of solidarity with what you're going through, do an internet search for "best divorce movies" and laugh along with all your favorite Hollywood actors as they bumble through this ridiculous process. There are plenty of movies out there. You may be able to laugh when you see others going through the same situation when you couldn't bring yourself to smile about it before. The more serious you consider a situation, the more power it has to stress you out. Laughing is a powerful medicine right now.

K is for Kisses

Did you know you can experience that "first kiss" again? When you're ready, and when the sparks are right, you'll experience the meeting of your lips on new ones. You'll get to feel those schoolyard butterflies in your stomach. It might be awkward. Your lips might be dryer than you'd like. You might say something dorky right afterward. Laugh it off as you soak up the new, weird energy. Be in that moment and let yourself take a chance again. Don't worry about where it will lead or how it will end, just savor the moment when it happens. Every person in this world has something different to offer. Their unique chemistry will blend with yours in ways you can't predict. It's possible that this kiss leads to the first, brave wildflowers cautiously pushing up through the scorched earth of your heart.

You may someday end up with another trusted life partner, you may not, but please enjoy this simple, fizzy, silly, lovely kiss.

L is for Loneliness

Those inside jokes you'd built up with your ex are useless now. You have an entire vocabulary that evolved for the two of you, and you find yourself sometimes referencing your inside jokes with oblivious outsiders. In these moments, the loneliness will hit you with intensity. In these moments, you realize it will be a long time if ever that you develop another unique language with another human. It might feel like you're going to die from the loneliness, but when that feeling hits, place your hand on your heart and feel it beating inside your core. Yep, everything is still ticking. You will go on.

M is for Money

Why can't you stop thinking about this? With everything else going on now, you also have to worry about which brand of peanut butter at the store fits best with your smaller budget. You announce to your extended family at holidays that your "presence will be the present" as you can't afford to shower everyone with gifts this year. You want to create space from your ex, but the money issue looms seemingly indefinitely. Is there child support you need to renegotiate? Alimony questions? Joint investments that you've been unable to liquidate? Enough already! You just want a clean break from this person.

When summer arrives, the home thermostat is kept at the highest bearable temperature instead of your crisp prefered setting. Goodness, do you miss that joint bank account, but staying married just for the financial security wasn't an attractive option. Now it's time to prove what you're worth. And guess what? You're worth a lot, so get that hustle on and get to work because next summer will be here before you know it and you're definitely not interested in this daily bargaining with your thermostat.

N is for Noise

You can't manage all the noise in your head some days. You're just trying to fill the car with gas, but your thoughts are running a mile a minute. Replaying a conversation. Thinking about your last wedding anniversary and how handsome he looked in that navy shirt you picked out for him. Whoops, I just used the Starbucks gift card instead of the credit card to try and pay... Imagining the what-ifs. Wondering if it's too soon for you to get involved with that cutie from the party. Did I really just select "diesel" for the gas? Cancel, let's try this again. Thinking of things to post on social media to trick everyone into thinking you're not a total trainwreck. You are thinking of everything except the task at hand. You drive off with the gas cap still open but won't notice until your next fill-up because your brain is so full of chatter, static and wild ideas that current reality barely registers.

When the noise becomes too much to bear, ground yourself. Find something in your immediate present on which you can focus. Take five deep breaths. Look outside your window to see the tree leaves shifting in the sunlight. Sing your favorite song. Turn off the devices. Bring yourself into the current moment if you can, but like so many things right now, time is ultimately the most effective tool to quiet the storm.

O is for Oasis

Create a space of refuge for yourself. Whether your space is on someone else's couch or you've got your own place, do what you need to create one tiny spot of this universe that's uniquely yours and provides you ultimate comfort. Shop for a new blanket or pillow that makes you feel decadent. Stream music in your space that calms your mind. Have an air freshener with a scent that reminds you of your favorite vacation destination. Buy a decoration that is a lovely place to rest your eyes. Create a piece of art or write some meaningful words on a piece of paper to display where you can see it daily. As much as possible, make a space that speaks to you.

If you still live in the home you shared with your ex and struggle living around reminders of your time together, try simply rearranging the furniture to see if you can get a fresh perspective on your environment. A few low-budget swaps like new dinner plates, sheets, fresh bathroom towels or updated curtains can be a small visual reminder that this is now exclusively your domain. In this castle you are King.

P is for Pacing

Yes, you've got big dreams of how to turn this warehouse full of lemons into lemonade. You know you want to move past this. You want to skip to the happy ending. But every amazing movie plot takes time, development, nemeses, and snags. You wouldn't want to watch a movie that just skipped to the last scene where to hero finally vanquishes the foe and manages to seal the kiss, would you? Accept the pace of your story. Imagine the plot of your life is being directed by an overeager Hollywood director and there are going to be a lot of dramatic moments - hopefully, less alien invasions, but hey, you never know. You can expect a few rough years facing all the pitfalls and setbacks that true heroes face.

Just like in the movies, everything you overcome brings you one step closer to resolution, though the process to get there may seem agonizingly slow. Some days you'll feel like you've been kicking forever upward through the water and your breath is almost exhausted. Please know the day really is coming that you'll finally break through the surface with a gasp and feel that sweet sunlight and warm air on your face. It's coming but for now, accept the timeline of this process if you can. While all the other elements to your life right now may seem unpredictable, time is the one thing you can count on. It will pass.

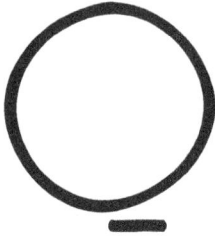

O is for Questions

Your kids want to know what went wrong. Your parents want to know if you need financial assistance. Your friends want to know who you're dating. The drunk guy at the bar wants to know how much money you ended up with. So many questions. And guess what? You don't have to answer any of them. Just like that. A smile, a hug, a "I'm glad to know you care, I'm sorting through a lot right now, and I'll let you know if I need anything," will suffice. People want you to know that they care about you, and sometimes the only way they know how to do this is to ask personal questions. Return their love but don't be their puppet. Answer the questions you're comfortable with if you choose, but never give away your right to privacy. And honestly, you won't have the answer to all these questions. Will you be able to keep the dog? Thinking about that only stresses you out at this point. If someone continues to push for information, a great response is, "You know, in my situation and out of respect for my ex, it's just smarter for me to keep private matters private. I hope you can understand." Manage a polite smile and change the subject. "Man, did you see on the news today about that guy going around licking people's doorbells? Crazy, huh?"

R is for Restraint

You've just mashed out an angry text to your ex in the heat of the moment, and your finger is hovering over the Send button. Pause. Read the message over and consider its long-term impact. Could this be used against you in legal proceedings? Are you saying what you mean or what you feel? After a few moments of thought, you usually don't send this sort of text. You're learning the wisdom of not fighting battles that can only be lost. Self-defense is a powerful emotion that can cause you to grab the phone to launch a verbal attack but take a deep breath and put the phone down. Strap on your boxing gloves and take it out on the punching bag in the garage instead.

Practice restraint in saying anything negative to your children about your ex. Your kids didn't sign divorce papers and deserve the right to their own unbiased opinions based on their unique relationship with each parent. When your ex knocks on the door to pick up yet more paperwork from you, pause before opening the door. Inhale deeply and smooth that bitter look off your face. Greet them with civil courtesy. The bloodiest part is over, and you're living your own life at this point. Now you get to practice becoming a Zen Warrior.

S is for Single

The grass may always be greener on the other side, but heavens, there are so many perks to this single thing! Do you want to fart under the bedroom blanket? Use up all the hot water during your shower? Make microwave s'mores for dinner? The position of the toilet seat is now under your absolute power. Even if you're actively trying to couple up, look for those silver linings until you do. Do you want to declare your home a beer, football and Michael Buble-free zone? Do you want to decorate your walls with heavy metal concert posters, neon bar signs or your ukulele collection? Do you want to wear that outfit you love that your ex always told you made you look fat or parade around in socks with sandals? Guess what, Champ? Go for it! There's no such thing as bad style right now, just your style!

If someone asks you if you're single, just say
yes! No need to duck your head shamefully
and mutter about how you're newly divorced.
Of course, you won't lie if they ask if you've
been married. If the relationship develops this
detail will certainly emerge, but embrace your
relationship status as single rather than divorced.
The first can provide you a sense of freedom.
The latter may carry a sense of failure that ties
you to the past.

T is for Tinder

Yes, it's great to meet new people right now, and swipe dating apps might appear to be a tantalizingly easy way to do this. Trust me, very soon after you start swiping, you'll begin seeing humanity differently and start to feel gross about not just the people on the apps but about yourself. You are more than a swipe. They are more than a height or a gym selfie. Now is not the time to minimize yourself or the amazing people you hope to meet. You may be emotionally fragile and susceptible right now. Unfortunately, some people will pounce on the opportunity to take advantage of that so go cautiously into the world of dating. Instead of installing a swipe dating app, show up single to the local dance bar and try line or swing-dancing to meet possible partners.

Tell friends you'd like to meet new people and have them introduce you to their social groups. Great partners are great friends; join a baking class, hiking club; any activity that allows men and women with similar interests to start filtering into your life. Even if you don't find someone to date right away, you're probably going to start making some friends and may even decide this is what you need more at this point. Ultimately, the biggest lesson you'll learn from swipe-dating apps is no amount of casual sex makes this hurt less.

U is for Underwear

Get some new ones! You need all the support you can get right now, so why not have some clothes that make you feel sexy and fresh again? Leather? Lace? Something to show off your assets? Go for it. Take that extra second to check yourself out in the mirror after you get dressed and give yourself a wink. One of life's simple mercies is that a new set of clothes really can make you feel like a new person. New clothes hold no ties to the past and set the stage for the future you're moving into. Spend a little extra money on styles or colors that you wouldn't have chosen in the past. Experiment with some new trends or hairstyles. Did your ex always make fun of how you looked in leather jackets? It seems like a good time to finally buy one for yourself, right? Don't worry about how it might look to someone else, just decide what you like on you. Never underestimate the power of looking sharp!

Hopefully, this means you can clean some other items out of your closet that tug your brain into painful memories of the past. That wedding dress can be resold or donated. The scarf your ex bought you on your birthday can be given to the homeless woman on the corner. Ask yourself which items in your closet do you more harm than good, and then allow yourself to let them go to make room for the new.

V is for Victories

Keep a victory list because--believe it or not--you're going to start racking up wins left and right! Finally agreed on custody arrangements? Victory! Finally had the divorce decree approved by the court? Victory! Finally figured out how the hell to put the artificial Christmas tree together on your own? Victory! Finally made it one whole day without looking your ex up on social media? Victory!

Good grief, you're just one huge sack of wins, aren't you? Everybody loves a winner and baby, you are on fire! It's painfully easy to focus on all the things falling apart right now so make an effort to notice those wins. They're all around if you start looking for them. In the past, your ex had always grilled the steaks, but the first time you light up that barbecue and grill your own dinner without catching your face on fire go ahead and take a victory selfie with your perfectly medium-rare ribeye. Set it as your screen saver as a reminder of what a total boss you are.

W is for Wishing

No amount of wishing will double your bank account. You can wish you were in your 20's again and had a do-over all day long; it won't make it happen. You know what wishes lead to? Nothing. Goals, plans, however, that's the mental fodder that will help you right now. So if you have that wish in your heart of what you want your life to look like, sit down with a piece of paper, your calendar, and make a plan. Set deadlines. Write out action steps. Make the phone calls and set the appointments. Soon what started as an empty wish will develop into a vibrant reality. Always beware of a wish that you can't make a plan for. That's the wish that's holding you back from the life you could be creating.

X is for Xanax

It's okay. You might need a little extra help to cope right now. Be honest with how your head is in your current moment. Despite all your best efforts, is your brain stuck in an endless rut of recurring thoughts, panic attacks, and self-destructive ideas? Needing a pill today doesn't mean you'll need one forever, but it's a miracle that there may be a tool out there that really can help you get back to just being able to smile. Divorce is a massively traumatic emotional event and can literally change your brain chemistry. There's no shame in letting medical advances or professional counselors balance the ship while you ride out the storm. Smiling feels good; you deserve that. Talk to a health professional and hopefully that therapist you hired when you moved out, and utilize the mental health resources available to help you move forward. The morning when you wake up and find yourself smiling for no reason while putting your socks on is coming, and it's going to be so deliciously lovely. Please don't give up on rediscovering this version of you.

Y is for Yes

What can you say "yes" to today? Can you take that road trip with a friend this weekend? Yes! Can you help out at that blood draw down at the community center? Yes! Take a long look at what you've been saying "no" to, and consider writing a more fulfilling life story through the vehicle of "yes." Do you want to discover what you're capable of? Maybe this is the year to finally flex your physical and emotional muscles in the desert with the Burning Man community or join your local theater group. Where will "yes" take you? Can you finally say yes to following your passion? Changing your career? Wearing white after Labor Day? Growth and change happen in the world of yes.

Z is for Zero

Zero need to conform to anyone's advice on how you should be living your life right now. Zero tolerance for letting yourself getting sucked back into old, destructive habits. Zero desire to compromise who you are as a person for the sake of other's comforts. You're smart enough to learn from the past and know that you're not back at the beginning again. You've leveled up and find yourself equipped with more smarts, skills, and mental inventory than ever before. Zero need to repeat past mistakes, my friend. The life you want to create is waiting for you to step up and take enthusiastic ownership whenever you're ready. This is your time.

About the Author

Sarah Flake is a professional health and weight loss coach and amateur over-sharer. She became fascinated with the power of words in Mr. Moses's third-grade class and is always amazed at the positive impact we can have on each other with loving, honest communication. Sarah is a firm believer that the more of our stories we share, the stronger we become as a community and attempts to help people get more comfortable with their "weird" side. She currently lives in Las Vegas, Nevada and strives daily to keep cacti, cats, and kids alive in her small but mighty home.

You can keep up with Sarah and her current and future projects at www.sarahflake.com.

About the Illustrator

Annie Poon is a multimedia artist living in Manhattan.

She makes everything from music to animation.

When Annie was little, she lived in the woods. She studied the animals and their wondrous ways. Her teachers took her to New York City to see the artwork of great masters. Annie wanted to be one of them. So she studied painting at the School of Visual Arts in Manhattan. But Annie found that childlike wonder and doodly explorations were more her thing. One of her animations, inspired by her childhood, is in the permanent collection of the Museum of Modern Art. Who would have thunk it? Annie is also a great letter writer and one of the only people in the world who still writes snail mail. She is 41. Sarah is her younger sister.

Acknowledgments

So many thanks to my mother, Barbara Benac (aka "The Editor") for her time, thoughtful comments and extensive grammatical corrections to take this publication from a scrawling, rant into an intelligible composition fit for tea time. Also, thanks to my daughters Penelope and Charlotte for encouraging me to share my thoughts and for providing the motivation for me to attempt the most amicable divorce and separation process possible. I strive daily to have my title of "mother" mean something beautiful to you both. I'm so thrilled I could finally collaborate with my brilliant sister Annie Poon on this project and see her charming illustrations bring my vision come to life. Hopefully, this is the first of many projects we create together. To all my amazing friends who have wiped my tears, bought me coffee, taken me dancing, and protected my heart during my own divorce process, I fully understand what a precious gift your friendship is. When I needed someone to call during my low moments, I never wondered who would care and you came through for me. It is quite a thing to understand that you are loved and I truly do. Thank you from the bottom of my heart.